Lights
in the Mine

DANGER
KEEP OUT!

Story by Sally Odgers
Illustrated by Liz Alger

Alfonso's Farm

Mines

Bulls' paddock

Barn

House

Contents

CHAPTER 1
Cold Air

Cold air breathed from the old mine tunnel, like smoke from a dragon's throat. Tim shivered and wrinkled up his face. His skin felt chilled, as if he had been leaning over an open deep-freeze.

"That mine is creepy!" said Jamie. She sounded pleased. Interested.

"Creepy or not," said Alfonso Tonelli, "stay *out* of the mines." He pointed to a sign on a nearby tree. "DANGER KEEP OUT! I put this sign up a month ago to keep the Beales boys from poking about."

"We wouldn't go in anyway," urged Tim. "Would we, Jamie?"

His sister frowned. "Oh, Grandpa! There might be lots of stuff in there!"

"There's nothing but mud and dust," said Alfonso. "So stay out."

Tim nodded. He was grateful to their grandfather for being stern. Otherwise Jamie would have nagged Tim to explore the mines with her.

"Jamie?" said Alfonso.

"All right," replied Jamie. "Who are the Beales boys?"

"Two young men with a lot of ideas and not much sense," said Alfonso. His face relaxed into a smile. "What shall we cook for lunch?"

"Pasta!" said Tim. "With mushrooms!" Alfonso made wonderful pasta. He had once owned an Italian restaurant, but had sold it and bought himself a little hillside property, stocked with Hereford cattle.

Alfonso had bought his farm cheaply because of the abandoned shale mines. Alfonso planned to fill them in one day. So far he hadn't had time, which was why the biggest mine was open, breathing cold air in the faces of Tim and Jamie.

CHAPTER 2
The Rules

After lunch, Alfonso said Jamie and Tim could go exploring. "Here are the rules," he said. "Stay away from the bulls. Don't move hay in the barn. And *don't* go into the mines up on the hill."

Tim wanted to look at the calves, but Jamie preferred to go and see the bulls.

"Grandpa said to stay away from them," protested Tim.

"We won't go into the paddock," said Jamie impatiently. "Don't be a chicken."

Jamie's pointed, freckled face looked stubborn. Tim knew if he refused to go, she'd sulk, so he followed her to the paddock. There were two dark-red bulls, with white faces and short curved horns.

"Mooo!" said Jamie, leaning against the fence.

"Don't do that," said Tim nervously. "They might not like it."

One bull stared at Jamie with small dark eyes and took a few steps toward the fence. Tim pulled Jamie away.

The bull lost interest and went back to eating grass.

"They're as tame as tame," said Jamie, sounding almost disappointed. "Come on, Tim, let's go to the barn."

"We're not to move the hay," reminded Tim. "It might fall on us."

Jamie jammed her fists on her hips. "Tim, do you *have* to be such a chicken?"

"I'm not," protested Tim. "I'm being cautious."

"Cautious!" Jamie sounded scornful. "That's just another word for chicken!"

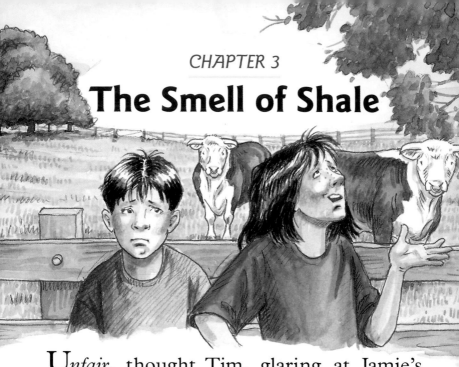

CHAPTER 3
The Smell of Shale

Unfair, thought Tim, glaring at Jamie's back when she had turned away. *It's just because she's older.*

For once, this thought didn't satisfy him. What if he felt the same when he was as old as Jamie? Even if he were braver by then, Jamie would still be older.

Anyway, thought Tim, *careful is good.* Careful keeps you out of trouble.

"Hey, Jamie," he called. "Let's look at the calves!"

But Jamie twitched her shoulders and ignored him.

Fine! thought Tim, *I'll do things on my own.* So he went and watched the calves, and then hunted a cricket chirping in the grass.

After a while, Jamie stopped sulking and went to find Tim. "Let's go up to the hill," she said in quite a friendly tone.

"No," said Tim. "The mines are up there. Besides, I'm busy. I'm looking for a cricket."

"You won't catch any crickets," said Jamie. "They always know exactly where you are. Come on, Tim! We won't go into the mines, just look around a bit."

Tim considered sulking too, but what was the point? He scrambled up and rubbed his knees, patterned from kneeling in the grass.

"The amazing decorated boy," teased Jamie as they went up the hill.

The three mine tunnels were all that was left of the shale oil company that had closed many years before. Two were small ventilation holes, but the one near the sign was as tall as Jamie and wider than Tim's outstretched arms.

They stood at the entrance again, as they had done that morning. Cold air breathed from the mouth of the mine.

Tim wrinkled his nose. "Why does it smell like railway stations?"

"It smells like that coal tar soap Grandpa uses," said Jamie.

"There wouldn't be soap inside a mine," said Tim.

"No trains, either!" said Jamie. "It must be the shale."

They edged closer, sniffing. The smell wasn't really unpleasant, just bitter and odd. The rocks around the entrance of the mine were dark and oily-looking and when Jamie picked one up, it crumbled in her hand.

She found a pebble and tossed it into the darkness.

"Don't do that!" exclaimed Tim as the pebble skipped and rattled.

"I'm trying to hit that shiny thing," said Jamie.

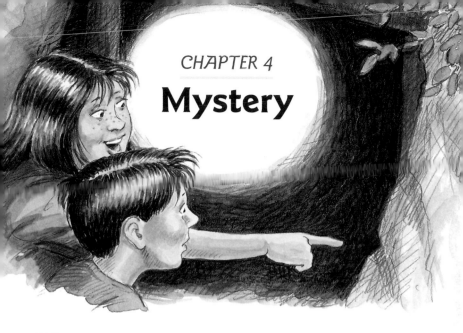

CHAPTER 4
Mystery

Tim peered past his sister. "I can't see anything shiny."

"Yes you can – look!" Jamie pointed into the darkness.

"Maybe it's silver or something," suggested Tim.

They squinted into the half-darkness. "I could nearly reach it," said Jamie.

"We're not to go in," Tim said.

"I'm not going in, silly," said Jamie. "Hand me that stick."

Armed with a long, thin stick, Jamie finally managed to drag it into the open. "Here it comes…" she reported. "Oh!" Her voice sank in disappointment. "It's not silver."

Tim held out his hand for the small object. "It's a battery!" he said, surprised. "And I can see something else."

It took a while to extract the second object from the mine. It was muddy and mostly black, which is why they hadn't noticed it before.

"It's a little garden fork," said Tim, frowning. "How odd."

"Very odd," said Jamie. "I wonder if it's Grandpa's?"

"Grandpa wouldn't go into the mine," said Tim. "And the sign keeps other people out."

"Someone must have gone into the mine," said Jamie. "Unless they just threw their garbage into the tunnel."

"This fork isn't garbage," pointed out Tim. "It's not broken, or even rusty."

"A fork and a battery," said Jamie, eyes sparkling. "This is a real mystery!"

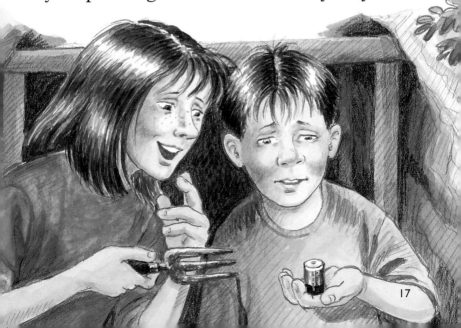

"We'd better tell Grandpa," said Tim.

"No," said Jamie, "let's try to solve it ourselves."

The mystery kept Jamie interested for the rest of the day.

"Maybe it's thieves, and they've stashed their loot in the mine!" she suggested.

"Grandpa hasn't mentioned any robberies," said Tim.

"Maybe it's treasure hunters, then," said Jamie. "Or maybe someone has buried something in there."

"Like what?" asked Tim nervously.

"Oh, like really old fossils. The sort of thing scientists dig up."

"We ought to tell Grandpa," insisted Tim.

"Chicken," said Jamie.

"Grandpa won't like strange people creeping about his farm," Tim worried.

"Maybe they did whatever they did a long time ago," Jamie argued.

Tim shook his head. There had been no rust on the things from the mine.

"I'll keep watch," said Jamie, but it was Tim who found the final clue to the mystery.

CHAPTER 5
Midnight

Jamie kept watch for the rest of the day and late into the evening, but she became tired and decided to go to bed.

"It's too late," she said. "Nobody's coming now."

Tim slept, too, but near midnight he woke and lay listening to the sounds of the night. One of the bulls bellowed, loud above the constant chirping of crickets. A dog barked in the distance.

Just then, a car drove up to the farm gate. Tim sat up and watched as the headlights swung past, then slowed and stopped. Strange. Alfonso's house was the only one here, and who could be calling on him so late at night? Tim slid out of bed and went to peer out the window. He was just in time to see the car lights dim and the dark outline fade into the night.

Tim held his breath, hearing the faint clunk of a door and then the crunch of footsteps. He narrowed his eyes, trying to make out the figures passing the house. They were sneaking along, carrying something large and bulky. Tim's breath caught with fear. He wanted to burrow back under the bedclothes, but what if they really were thieves?

Tim hurried to the next room where Jamie was sleeping. "Jamie!" He shook his sister's shoulder. "Come and look!"

"Huh?" said Jamie sleepily.

"Thieves!" whispered Tim. "Or something."

Jamie scrambled out of bed and ran to her window, but by now the feet had crunched beyond hearing, and the dark figures had disappeared.

"You imagined it," said Jamie. "Or else you were dreaming." She went back to bed, but Tim stayed crouched by the window.

The bull bellowed again, and a night bird cried out over the hill. And Tim saw a flicker of light in the distance. It flitted among the trees, then settled like a firefly.

Someone had a flashlight out there, and Tim was sure it was shining into the mine.

CHAPTER 6

Someone at the Mine

"Jamie!" called Tim. "Come quick! Somebody's over at the mine!"

Grumbling, Jamie came back to the window. "I *told* you, Tim..." Her voice trailed off as Tim pointed. The light gleamed for another few seconds, then the dark seemed to swallow it. "You were right," said Jamie, excitedly. "There's someone in the mine. Let's go!"

"No," said Tim. "Don't be stupid. I'm going to wake Grandpa."

"You already have," said a deep voice, and Alfonso appeared. "What's going on?"

"There's someone at the mine," said Tim excitedly.

"They're digging for treasure," added Jamie. "They left a fork behind before."

"*And* a battery," said Tim.

"Hmm," said Alfonso. "A fork and a battery, you say?"

Then Alfonso sighed. "I suspect I know who it is, but I don't know what they're up to," he said. "Put your jackets on while I get dressed."

Jamie and Tim stared at one another.

"We can come *too*?" squeaked Tim.

"If you want to," said Alfonso. "They may as well see who spotted them."

"Tim's too chicken," said Jamie.

"No, I'm not!" said Tim boldly. "I really want to come!"

It was strange, creeping through the dark. Alfonso had brought a powerful flashlight with them, but didn't switch it on, even when they arrived at the mine.

A dim light was shining out of the mouth, and they could hear a faint murmur of voices.

"It's perfect, Nick!" said one. "Look at the little beauties!"

"Let's hope the old man doesn't find out," said his companion.

"Why should he, Nick? He won't even know we've been here."

Alfonso cleared his throat. "The old man *does* know you're here," he said sternly, "and the old man is *not pleased*."

Silence.

"Uh-oh," said a voice from the mine.

CHAPTER 7
Mystery Solved

"Come out!" ordered Alfonso, and he switched on his flashlight.

Tim and Jamie held their breath as two young men crept sheepishly out of the tunnel. One clutched a sack, the other a basket full of round things that gleamed in the flashlight.

"Loot!" gasped Jamie, but Tim was closer and saw what was in the basket.

"No," he said, holding back a grin. "Mushrooms!"

"Nick and Toby Beales!" said Alfonso, glaring at the young men. "I told you to stay away from these mines, remember?"

"We're only growing mushrooms," said Nick.

"The mine's a perfect place for it," said Toby. "Damp and dark."

"We weren't doing any harm," muttered Nick.

"That's not the point, you stupid boys!" roared Alfonso. "The sign doesn't say DANGER for nothing. There'll be *real* trouble if I catch you here again!"

The mushroom farmers jumped at Alfonso's roar, and Toby dropped his basket.

"How did you know we were here?" he asked nervously.

"You left a fork and a battery behind," said Tim. "I suppose the battery was out of your flashlight."

"And tonight we saw the lights in the mine," said Jamie.

"You mean, it was you kids who tracked us down?" wailed Toby.

"It certainly was!" said Alfonso. "They're sharper than you, so from now on, stay away!"

The Beales boys scurried away.

"What now?" asked Jamie, yawning.

"Back to bed," said Alfonso. He started to head down the hill, but suddenly stopped. He grinned and picked up the basket Toby had dropped. "Someone seems to have left us a basket of mushrooms! What do you say to frying a few for our breakfast in the morning?"

"Mushrooms. My favorite!" Tim grinned. "Solving mysteries is hungry work!"